Trumpeter Swan

The World's Largest Waterbird

by Leon Gray

Consultant: John E. Cornely PhD
The Trumpeter Swan Society

BEARPORT PUBLISHING

New York, New York

Credits

Cover, © Ray Wilson/Alamy; TOC, © SF photo/Shutterstock; 4–5, © Malcolm Schuyl/FLPA; 6, © Steve Oehlenschlager/123RF.com; 8T, © Nancy Bauer/Shutterstock; 8B, © renamarie/123RF.com; 9, © Sue Robinson/Shutterstock; 10, © Thomas Mangelsen/Minden Pictures/FLPA; 11, © Lynn M. Stone/Naturepl.com; 12, © Tom Mangelsen/Naturepl.com; 13, © Michael Quinton/Minden Pictures/FLPA; 14–15, © Tom and Pat Leeson/ardea.com; 16, © operative401/Shutterstock; 17, © Gkuchera/Dreamstime.com; 18, © Steve Oehlenschlager/Shutterstock; 19, © Gkuchera/Dreamstime.com; 20–21, © George McCarthy/Naturepl.com; 22L, © Sue Robinson/Shutterstock; 22C, © Rich Lindie/Shutterstock; 22R, © iliuta goean/Shutterstock; 23BG, © Critterbiz/Shutterstock; 23TL, © operative401/Shutterstock; 23TR, © Holly Kuchera/Shutterstock; 23BL, © Steve Oehlenschlager/Shutterstock; 23BR, © Ron Rowan Photography/Shutterstock.

Publisher: Kenn Goin
Senior Editor: Joyce Tavolacci
Creative Director: Spencer Brinker
Photo Researcher: Calcium Creative

Library of Congress Cataloging-in-Publication Data

Gray, Leon, 1974-
 Trumpeter swan : the world's largest waterbird / by Leon Gray.
     pages cm. — (Even more supersized!)
 Audience: 6-9.
 Includes bibliographical references and index.
 ISBN 978-1-61772-734-4 (library binding) — ISBN 1-61772-734-2 (library binding)
 1. Trumpeter swan—Juvenile literature. I. Title.

 QL696.A52G73 2013
 598.4'184—dc23

                            2012035913

For more information, write to Bearport Publishing Company, Inc., 45 West 21st Street, Suite 3B, New York, New York 10010. Printed in the United States of America.

10 9 8 7 6 5 4 3 2 1

Contents

A Big Bird

The trumpeter swan is the world's largest **waterbird**.

A trumpeter swan can weigh more than 30 pounds (13.6 kg). That is about as much as a three-year-old child.

When the trumpeter swan's wings are spread out, they measure eight feet (2.4 m) from tip to tip. That is about as long as a small rowboat.

Swan Homes

Trumpeter swans live in parts of Canada and the United States.

Some stay in the same area all year round, while others **migrate**.

Swans that migrate spend the summer in cooler places that are farther north.

Then they fly south to spend the winter in places that are warmer.

Trumpeter swans fly north or south in groups called **flocks**.

Trumpeter Swans in the Wild

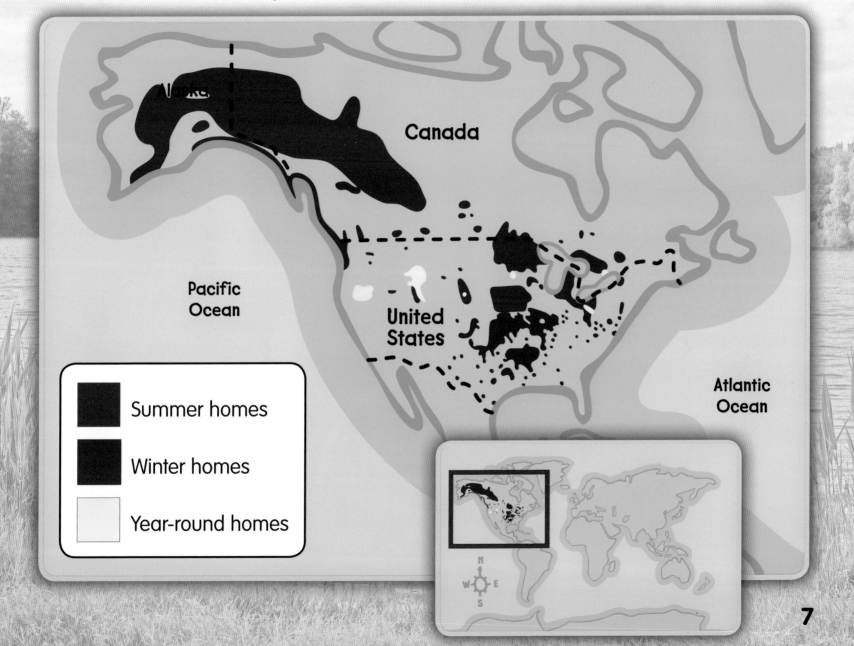

Alaska

Canada

Pacific
Ocean

United
States

Atlantic
Ocean

■ Summer homes

■ Winter homes

☐ Year-round homes

Black and White

Trumpeter swans are tall, graceful birds with long, thin necks.

Adults have black **beaks** and black legs and feet.

Their wide webbed feet are used for swimming.

The swans' bodies are covered with thick white feathers.

beak

webbed foot

There are two other kinds of swans that live in North America. They are mute swans and tundra swans. Both have white feathers, just like trumpeter swans.

male mute swan

female mute swan

Dipping for Dinner

Whether they migrate or not, trumpeter swans always live close to water.

They make their homes in or near marshes, rivers, ponds, or lakes.

Plants that grow in water are their main food.

As the big birds swim, they grab the plants with their beaks.

To reach underwater plants, they tip their bodies over so that their tails are showing.

In the water, trumpeter swans will also eat insects, snails, and other small animals. On land, they sometimes eat grasses.

Making a Nest

A male swan is called a cob, and a female is called a pen.

In the spring, pairs of cobs and pens get ready to have baby swans.

Together, they use water plants and sticks to build a huge nest.

When the nest is done, the pen lays between five and nine eggs inside it.

Then she sits on the eggs to keep them warm, while the cob guards the nest.

sticks

A trumpeter swan might build a nest on land near the water's edge or in shallow water.

13

Growing Up

After about 35 days, the swans' eggs hatch.

The fluffy gray babies that come out are known as cygnets.

Soon, they are able to follow their parents into the water to look for food.

At first, the babies eat mostly insects and snails.

After the cygnets are a few weeks old, they start eating plants.

Cygnets start out their lives with light gray feathers. They grow white feathers by the time they are one year old.

cygnets

Fighting Off Enemies

Because of their huge size, adult trumpeter swans do not have many enemies.

They can fight off most other animals with their strong wings and beaks.

However, coyotes, eagles, and owls hunt and eat cygnets.

To protect their babies, the parents threaten any hungry animal that gets too close.

They spread their huge wings and hiss loudly to scare the animal away.

strong beak

Trumpeter swans also make loud trumpet-like sounds. The large birds got their name from these calls.

Fly, Fly Away

Cygnets begin learning to fly when they are about four months old.

They practice by following their parents on short flights.

Over time, the flights become longer and longer.

In the fall, swans that migrate take off for a very long trip.

The young swans follow their parents south—to the place where they will spend the winter.

adult swan

young swan

Young trumpeter swans stay with their parents for about a year. They start their own families when they are about three or four years old.

Saving Swans

Trumpeter swans once lived in many parts of North America.

During the 1800s, however, hunters shot almost all of them for their feathers and meat.

The feathers were used to make pillows and women's hats.

Luckily, though, people passed laws to stop hunters from killing the birds.

As a result, more of these beautiful swans can again be seen in the wild.

In the past, only about 70 trumpeter swans could be found living in North America. Today, there are more than 46,000 of these swans.

21

More Large Waterbirds

Trumpeter swans are a kind of bird. All birds are warm-blooded, have feathers, and lay eggs. Most birds fly. A few, such as the ostrich and the penguin, cannot fly.

Here are three more large waterbirds.

Mute Swan

The mute swan is another heavy waterbird. It can weigh up to 27 pounds (12 kg). It is not really mute, or soundless, but the sounds it makes are not loud.

Albatross

Albatrosses can weigh up to 22 pounds (10 kg). These waterbirds are rarely seen on land and can glide for hours without rest.

White Pelican

The white pelican can weigh up to 20 pounds (9 kg). The bird can also hold up to three gallons (11.4 liters) of water in its large throat pouch.

Trumpeter Swan
30 pounds/13.6 kg

Mute Swan
27 pounds/12 kg

Albatross
22 pounds/10 kg

White Pelican
20 pounds/9 kg

Glossary

beaks (BEEKS) the hard, pointed parts of birds' mouths

migrate (MYE-grate) to move from one place to another at a certain time of year

flocks (FLOKS) groups of the same kind of bird that live or travel together

waterbird (WAW-tur-BURD) a bird that lives on or near water

23

Index

Read More

Bodden, Valerie. *Swans (Amazing Animals)*. Mankato, MN: Creative Education (2009).

Lawrence, Ellen. *A Bird's Life (Animal Diaries: Life Cycles)*. New York: Bearport (2013).

Mitchell, Susan K. *Things with Wings (Biggest vs. Smallest)*. Berkeley Heights, NJ: Enslow (2011).

Learn More Online

To learn more about trumpeter swans, visit
www.bearportpublishing.com/EvenMoreSuperSized